Butterflies

and other insects

Editor: Janine Amos
Designer: Ruth Hall

ISBN 0 361 06678 3

Published 1985 by Purnell Books, Paulton, Bristol BS18 5LQ
a member of the BPCC Group
Made and printed in Great Britain by Purnell
and Sons (Book Production) Limited, Paulton, Bristol
Phototypeset by Quadraset Limited

SPOT and STICK

Butterflies
and other insects

Robin Kerrod

Illustrated by
Alan Male

Purnell

Contents

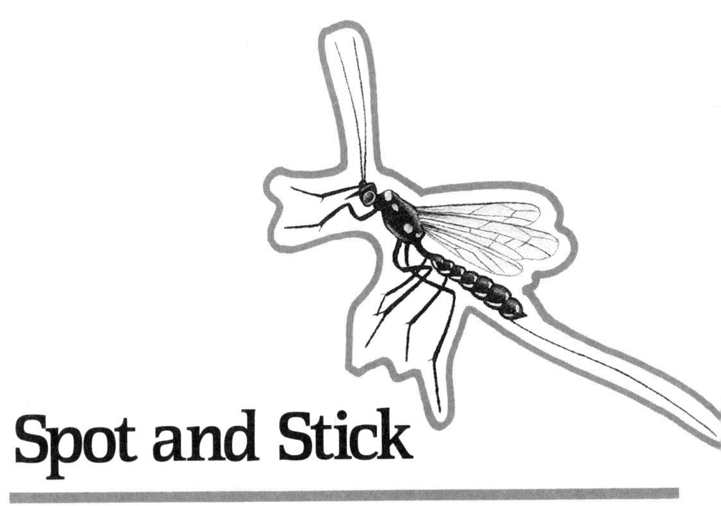

Spot and Stick

You will notice in the book that some insects have a star next to their names. This tells you that there are stickers for these insects. When you spot one, cut out the sticker and stick it in a suitable place on the frieze. You can either leave the frieze at the back of the book, or cut it out and stick it on the wall.

Introduction

You will have no trouble in finding plenty of insects. Many will probably find you! Insects are the most successful creatures that have ever lived on Earth. They are found on land and in water almost everywhere.

Some of the insects we see today first appeared on Earth over 300 million years ago. They include the tiny silverfish, which you find in every kitchen.

Altogether there are thought to be at least 2,000,000 kinds of insects in the world. In Britain alone there are more than 20,000 different kinds. They vary widely in shape, colour and size, but they do have certain features in common. In particular, their bodies are made of three parts, or segments, and they have six legs. Most insects have wings.

Using this Book

In this book we have divided up the insects into six groups. Butterflies; moths; beetles; bees, ants and wasps; flies; and other common insects. You can find out more about these groups on page 7.

When you spot an insect you want to identify, look at its shape and colouring. Then try to match these features with a picture in the book. Look first in the section you think covers the kind of insect you have found. The text gives more information to help you.

When insect-hunting, you may come across a caterpillar. This is an earlier stage in the life of a butterfly or moth. You may be able to identify the caterpillar from the pictures on pages 4 and 5.

The main insect names given in this book are the common names. Underneath are the scientific names, given in Latin. The first part of the Latin name gives the genus of the insect. This is the name of a group of similar insects. The second part of the Latin name gives the species of the insect. This refers to one particular kind of insect within the group.

Caterpillars of Butterflies

Caterpillars of Moths

The Insect Body

Insects belong to a large group of creatures without backbones, called invertebrates. The whole group have jointed legs, but only insects have just six legs. They also have a jointed body, made up of three parts. There is a head; a middle body, or thorax; and a rear body, or abdomen.

The two large eyes of an insect are different from our own eyes because they are made up of many lenses. They are called compound eyes. Often there are two simple eyes as well. The insect uses its feelers, or antennae, to feel and often to smell.

The thorax is made up of three parts, or segments. A pair of legs is attached to each one. Two pairs of wings are usually attached to the two segments at the rear. The abdomen of an insect is usually divided up into 10 segments. At the rear are the sex organs, which the insect uses for mating. Females have tiny tubes for laying eggs, called ovipositors.

Like all creatures, insects must breathe to live. But they breathe in a different way from most animals. They take in air through tiny air holes, or spiracles.

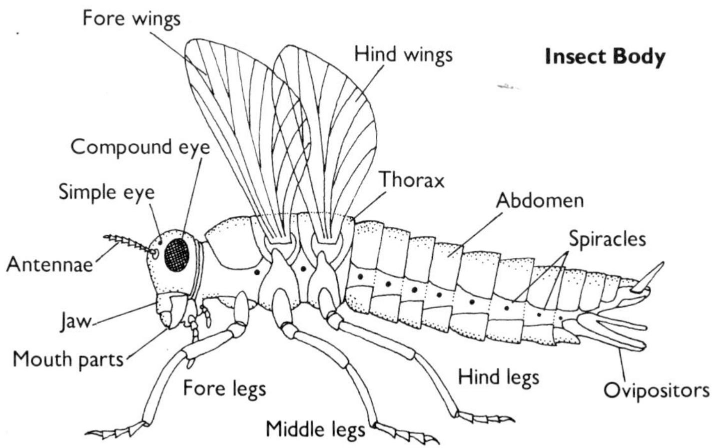

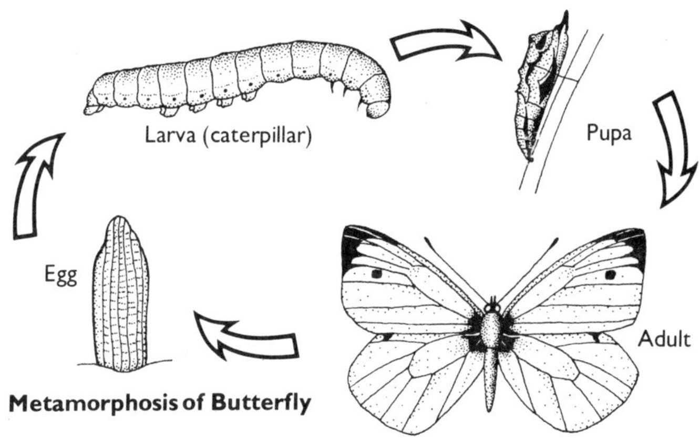

Metamorphosis of Butterfly

Insect Life Cycles

Insects begin life when eggs laid by the female hatch out. Usually they hatch into wriggling larvae, which are popularly called caterpillars, maggots or grubs. A larva eats and grows, and turns into another form, called a pupa, which has a hard shell. Inside the pupa the insect gradually changes into an adult.

This kind of life history, or life cycle, is called a metamorphosis. Some insects have a different life cycle of only three stages—egg, nymph and adult.

The Main Insect Groups

BUTTERFLIES and MOTHS belong to a large insect group, or order, called **Lepidoptera**. This means 'scale wings'. The dust that comes off on your fingers when you touch these insects is made up of scales.
BEETLES belong to the order **Coleoptera**, meaning 'sheath wings'. Instead of front wings, beetles have hard wing-cases, which protect the hind wings and body.
BEES, ANTS AND WASPS belong to the order **Hymenoptera**, meaning 'membrane wings'.
FLIES belong to the order **Diptera**, meaning 'two wings'. They have a single pair of wings. This order also includes gnats, mosquitoes and crane flies.

★

Red Admiral

Vanessa atalanta

Span: 6 cm

A common garden butterfly, often found in large numbers. The caterpillars feed on stinging nettles. Many red admirals fly south during the autumn, but some hibernate for the winter.

Orange Tip

Anthocharis cardamines

Span: 3.5 cm

The female does not have the bright orange tips to the forewings and looks rather like a small white. The caterpillars feed on such plants as hedge mustard and cuckoo flower.

★

Swallowtail

Papilio machaon

Span: 8 cm

This large and beautiful butterfly is rare in Britain, where it is found mainly in the Norfolk Broads. It is more common in mainland Europe, where it lives in open country.

Peacock

Inachis io

Span: 6 cm

This is another attractive common butterfly. It has four striking eye-spots on its wings, like those on the tail of a peacock. The caterpillars feed on stinging nettles. The butterflies are most common in the autumn and fly until they hibernate.

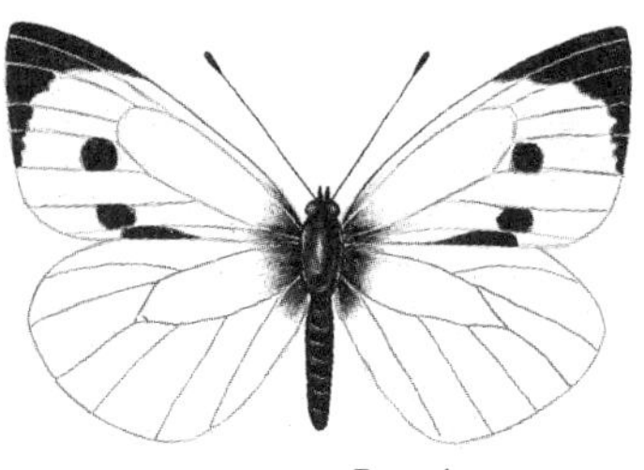

Female

Large White

Pieris brassicae

Span: 6 cm

This large, creamy-white butterfly feeds on plants of the cabbage family. The wings are yellower underneath. The female has two black spots on the forewings. The small white has similar markings, but has a span of only about 4.5 cm.

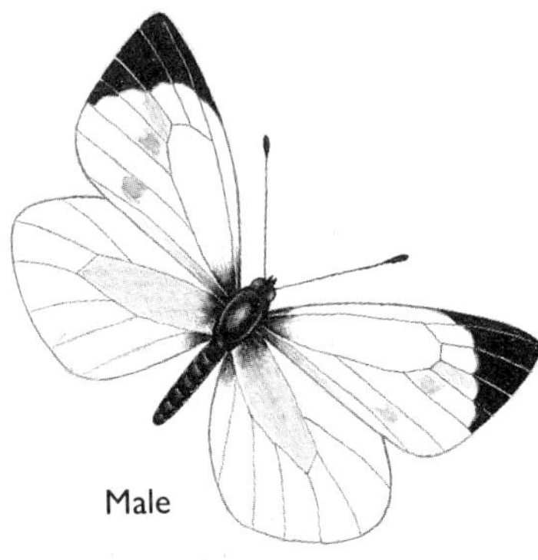

Male

Small Heath

Coenonympha pamphilus

Span: 3 cm

This butterfly is common and widespread. It is found on grasslands everywhere, and the caterpillars feed on grasses. It is orange-brown in colour, with dark spots on the forewings.

Silver-washed Fritillary

Argynnis paphia

Span: 7.5 cm

The silvery bands on the underside of the brownish hindwings give this butterfly its name. It lives in woods, and its caterpillars usually hibernate in bark. They feed on violet leaves in the spring. This is the largest of the group of mottled butterflies called fritillaries.

Marbled White

Melanargia galathea

Span: 5 cm

This is a striking dark brown and white butterfly of the meadows and chalky downs. Its caterpillars feed on tall grasses. The underwings are much paler and yellowish.

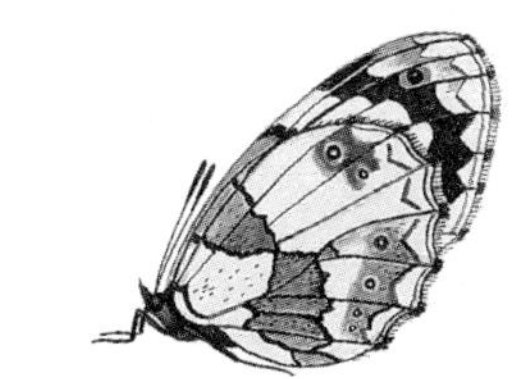

Small Tortoiseshell

Aglais urticae

Span: 5 cm

The small tortoiseshell is one of our commonest garden butterflies. The caterpillars feed on stinging nettles. The autumn butterflies hibernate, often in buildings.

Silver-spotted Skipper

Hesperia comma

Span: 3 cm

Like other skippers, this butterfly looks rather like a moth. It is named after the silvery-white markings on its greenish underwings. Also like other skippers, the male has black streaks on the forewings, which are scent scales.

Male

Painted Lady

Vanessa cardui

Span: 6.5 cm

Closely related to the red admiral, this colourful butterfly has similar white markings on the wing-tips. The caterpillars feed on thistles and stinging nettles. The butterflies mostly fly south for the winter.

Comma

Polygonia c-album

Span: 5 cm

This butterfly is named after the white comma mark on the underside of the hindwings. It is easily recognized by the ragged edges of the wings. Commas hibernate in the open, usually on branches.

White Admiral

Limenitis camilla

Span: 5.5 cm

This woodland butterfly was first called the white admirable. Its upperwings are dark brown and white, and its underwings are lighter in colour. The caterpillars feed on honeysuckle.

Wall Brown

Lasiommata megera

Span: 4.5 cm

This orange and brown butterfly can often be seen sunning itself on stones and walls. It has clear spots on the forewings and hindwings. The caterpillars feed on grasses.

Female

Purple Hairstreak

Quercusia quercus

Span: 3.5 cm

This butterfly is blackish in colour and flashes blue-purple as the light catches it. The male shows this all over, while the female does so only on parts of the forewings. It lives mainly in oak woods.

Meadow Brown

Maniola jurtina

Span: 5 cm

The meadow brown is darker brown and less mottled than the wall brown and does not have the spots on the hindwings. The caterpillars feed on grasses, usually at night.

Male

Female

Brimstone

Gonepteryx rhamni

Span: 5.5 cm

The brimstone is a yellow butterfly that lives in woodlands and hedgerows. The female is much paler and could be mistaken for a large white. The caterpillars feed on buckthorn. The butterflies hibernate during the winter, looking like pale leaves.

Small Copper

Lycaena phlaeas

Span: 2.5 cm

This is the most common and widespread of the coppers. These butterflies all have the coppery-orange colour with darkish markings. They are found on flowery banks and meadows. The caterpillars feed on the leaves of dock and sorrel.

Common Blue

Polyommatus icarus

Span: 3.5 cm

Male

The male is a fine, clear blue. The female is more brown than blue and has orange spots along the wing edges. Both are pale brown with orange tips underneath, like the chalk-hill blue. The caterpillars usually feed on vetch and clover.

Female

★

Chalk-hill Blue

Lysandra coridon

Span: 3.5 cm

This is a paler blue butterfly, which lives in chalk and limestone hilly regions. The female is mainly dark brown with only a hint of blue. Both sexes are pale brown underneath. The caterpillars feed only on horse-shoe vetch.

Male

White Ermine

Spilosoma lubricipeda

Span: 6 cm

This moth is nearly all white with black spots, mainly on the forewings. It flies mainly at night. The very hairy caterpillars move very quickly over the ground. They feed on plantains, dandelions and other low plants.

Buff-tip

Phalera bucephala

Span: 6 cm

The buff-tip is an attractive moth, with pale blue hindwings and silvery-grey and brown forewings. The yellowish tips of the forewings show when the moth is at rest and make it look like a broken branch. It is common in woodland.

Clouded Buff

Diacrisia sannio

Span: 6 cm

This brightly-coloured moth lives in heathland. The female is orange-brown with the wings outlined in red. The male is much paler. You can sometimes see it flying during the day. The female, however, does not fly until dusk.

Oak Eggar

Lasiocampa quercus

Span: 7.5 cm

This orange-brown moth has large spots on the forewings. The male is darker than the female and has plumed, or feathery antennae. Oak eggars can be found on the edges of woodlands and in the hedgerows. The caterpillars feed on bramble and hawthorn.

Female

Male

★

Eyed Hawkmoth

Smerinthus ocellata

Span: 8 cm

This beautiful moth is named after the large blue and black eyes on the pink hindwings. It shows these spots to frighten away attackers. The caterpillars feed on the leaves of sallow, willow and apple trees.

Six-spot Burnet

Zygaena filipendulae

Span: 4 cm

A brightly-coloured small moth commonly found in grasslands. Its colours warn attackers that it is unpleasant to eat. The caterpillars feed on vetches, clover and other trefoils. They spin their silky cocoons (in which the pupae form) high up on tall grasses.

★

Elephant Hawk-moth

Deilephila elpenor

Span: 6.5 cm

This colourful moth feeds at night from flowers, such as rosebay willowherb and marsh bedstraw. It feeds on their nectar through its long 'tongue', while hovering like a humming bird. It is named after the shape of its caterpillars, which look rather like an elephant's trunk.

★

Death's-head Hawkmoth

Acherontia atropos

Span: 11 cm

This moth takes its name from the skull-like markings on its back. It is one of the biggest of all moths. Unusually for an insect, it squeaks when alarmed! It does this by forcing air through its long 'tongue'. The caterpillars feed on the leaves of potato plants or woody nightshade.

Peppered Moth

Biston betularia

Span: 6 cm

These moths are often pepper-coloured and can also be found mainly black speckled with white, and even all black. In industrial regions the darker forms are common because they blend in with the grimy surroundings.

Magpie Moth

Abraxas grossulariata

Span: 4 cm

This moth is white speckled with black and yellow-orange. So are the caterpillars. It is also called the currant moth because the caterpillars eat the leaves of currant and gooseberry bushes.

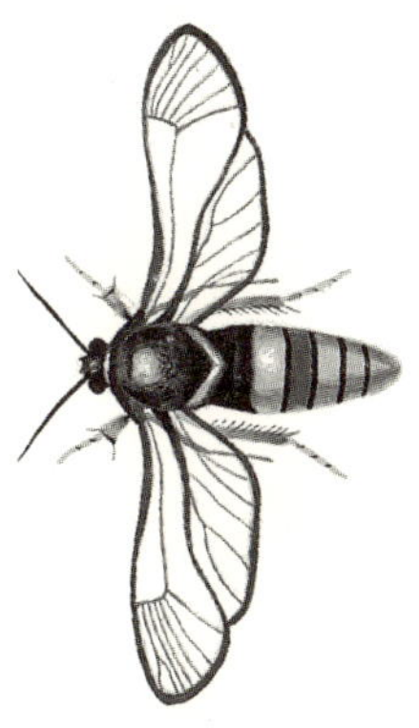

Hornet Moth

Sesia apiformis

Span: 4 cm

A good name because this moth does look like a hornet. It has a black and yellow striped body and transparent wings. The caterpillars feed on, and burrow into, the wood of poplars. They take up to three years to turn into moths.

Goat Moth

Cossus cossus

Span: 8.5 cm

A brownish-grey moth, whose caterpillars burrow into the wood of ash, elm, poplar and willow trees to feed. The caterpillars have an unpleasant smell, which gives the moth its name.

★
Garden Tiger

Arctia caja

Span: 7.5 cm

This moth is brown and white in its rest position, but when it is attacked, it shows the bright red-orange hindwings and a red 'collar'. The caterpillars feed on nettles, docks, dandelions and many other plants.

★
Large Emerald

Geometra papilionaria

Span: 5 cm

This beautiful moth is common in birch woods. In the spring it gradually turns green and becomes difficult to see among the leaves. Notice how the caterpillars loop their bodies while moving. They are called 'loopers'.

Horn-tail Ichneumon
Honey Bee drone
Wall Mason Wasp
Tiger Beetle
Seven-spot Ladybird
Cockchafer
Honey Bee queen
Death's Head Hawkmoth
Buff-tailed Bumblebee
Hornet
Glow-worm
Honey Bee worker

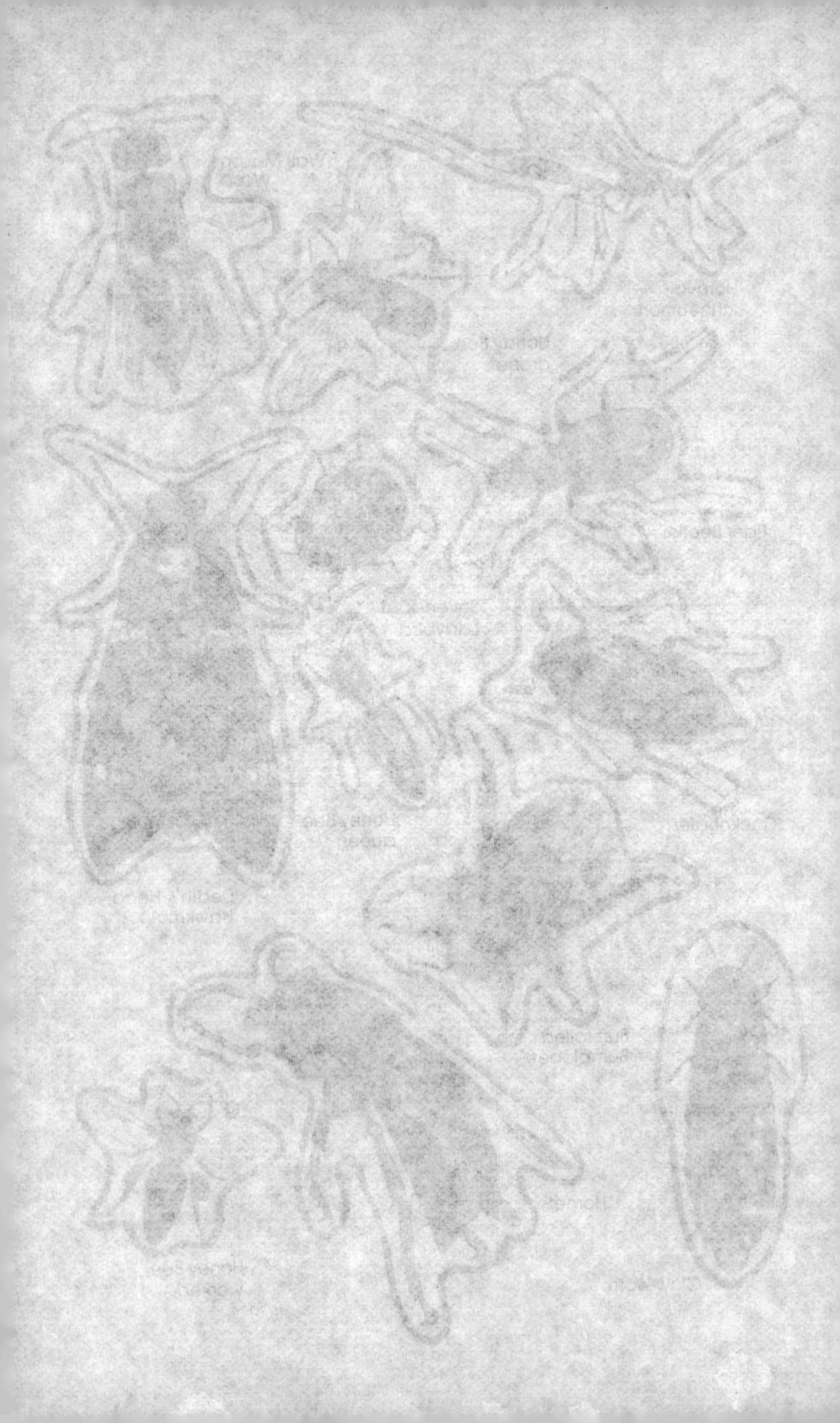

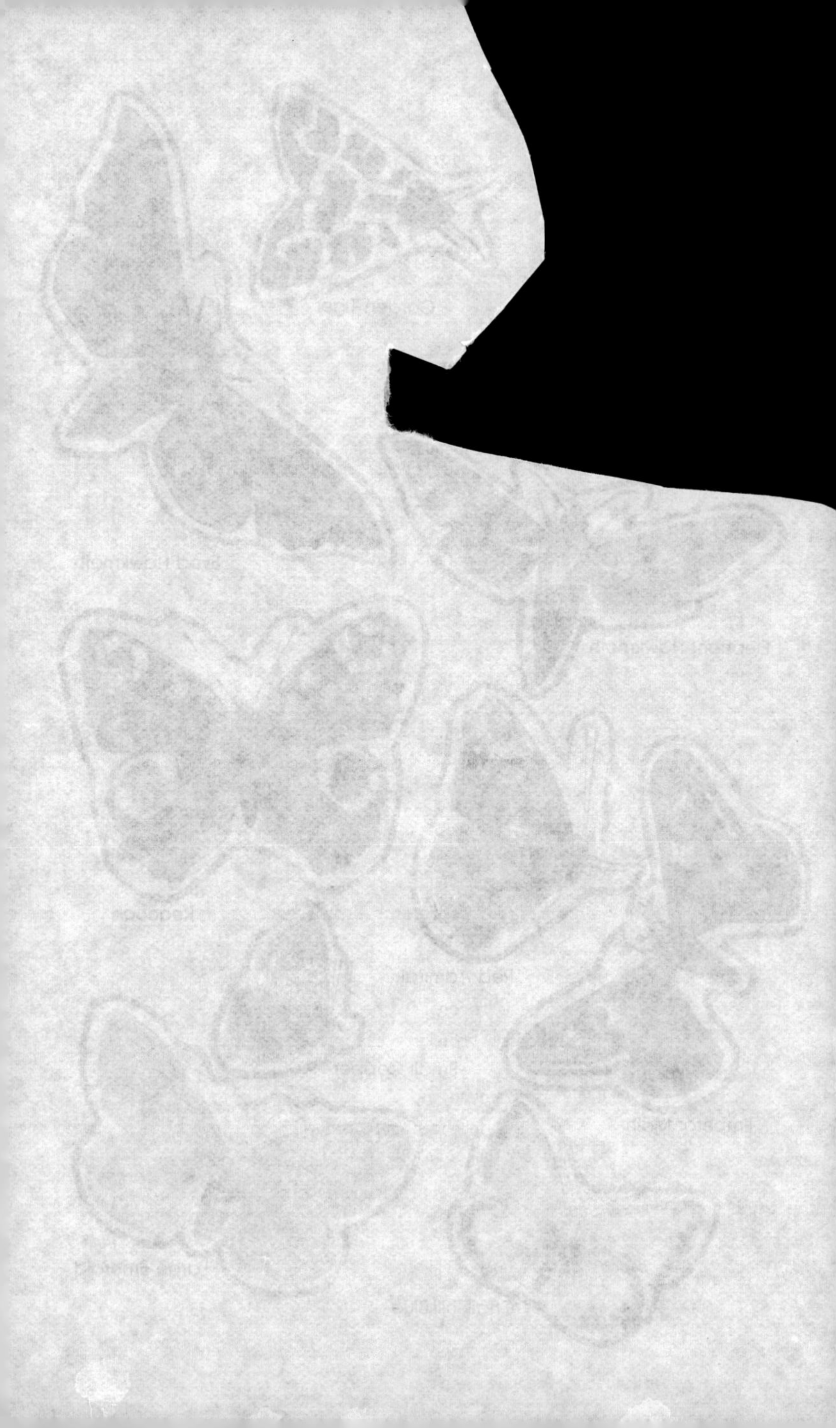

Garden Tiger
Eyed Hawkmoth
Elephant Hawkmoth
Peacock
Red Admiral
Small Copper
Emperor Moth
Large Emerald
Chalk-hill Blue

Swallowtail Moth

Ourapteryx sambucaria

Span: 5 cm

This is an unmistakable moth because of its 'tail'. Its eggs are scarlet in colour. Its caterpillars are twig-like and feed on the leaves of ivy, privet, oak and other trees. They hibernate in bark during the winter.

Male

★

Emperor Moth

Saturnia pavonia

Span: 7.5 cm

With large eye-spots on all four wings, the emperor moth cannot be mistaken. The female is much larger than the male and does not have the male's orange hindwings. The male flies by day, the female only at night.

Beetles

Whirligig Beetle

Gyrinus marinus

Length: 6 mm

Groups of these tiny, shiny black beetles can often be seen on the surface of ponds, swimming madly round and round.

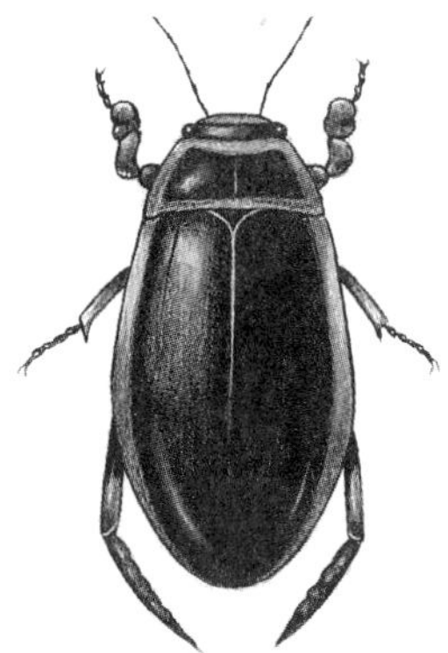

Giant Water Beetle

Dytiscus marginalis

Length: 35 mm

These common water beetles are brownish-black, and their hind legs are fringed with hairs. The male has sucker pads on its forelegs. The female has grooved wing-cases. They are also called great diving beetles.

Shiny Ground Beetle

Harpalus aenus

Length: 10 mm

A small beetle, whose shiny wing-cases are various shades of green, purple and bronze. The legs and antennae are reddish.

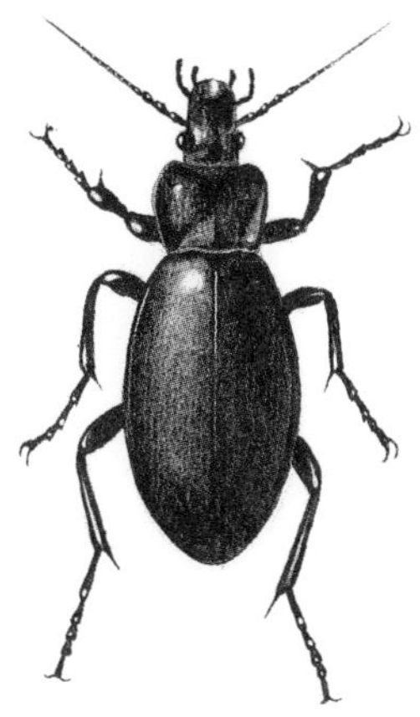

Ground Beetle

Carabus nemoralis

Length: 25 mm

This is also called the violet ground beetle. Its thorax (upper body part) is purplish, and the wing-cases are greenish-bronze. It is active at night.

Tanner Beetle

Prionus coriarius

Length: 40 mm

One of the biggest long-horn beetles, which are named after their long antennae. The tanner's antennae are saw-toothed. Its thorax has sharp spines each side.

Cellar Beetle

Blaps mucronata

Length: 25 mm

This is also called the churchyard beetle. It is a black, slow-moving beetle with an unpleasant smell, found in dark, damp places.

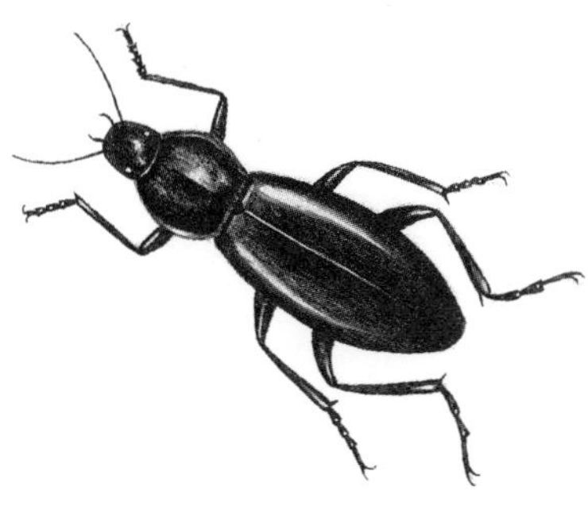

Common Burying Beetle

Necrophorus vespillo

Length: 20 mm

Another name for this insect is the sexton beetle. Several beetles together will bury the body of a small, dead animal, on which their grubs will feed. Notice the reddish-orange bands on the wing-cases.

Dung Beetle

Aphodius fimetarius

Length: 8 mm

This is one of 40 or more kinds of beetles that live on and in animal dung. They have reddish-brown wing-cases and are related to the chafers.

★

Cockchafer

Melolontha melolontha

Length: 25 mm

The cockchafer is often called a May bug, because it flies noisily on May evenings. Its larvae, or grubs can do serious damage to crops by attacking the roots.

Glow-worm

Lampyris noctiluca

Length: 20 mm

This beetle can be seen in the dark because it gives out a soft, greenish glow. The female is larger than the male and has no wings or wing-cases. It also has a brighter glow than the male.

Female

Seven-spot Ladybird

Coccinella 7-punctata

Length: 8 mm

This is just one of the many ladybirds found in Britain. Others are yellow with black spots and black with yellow spots. All are welcome in the garden because they feed on aphids.

Tiger Beetle

Cicindela campestris

Length: 15 mm

This beautiful ground beetle likes dry, sandy soils. It has green wing-cases, and long, powerful legs for running down its prey. You often see it flying about on sunny days.

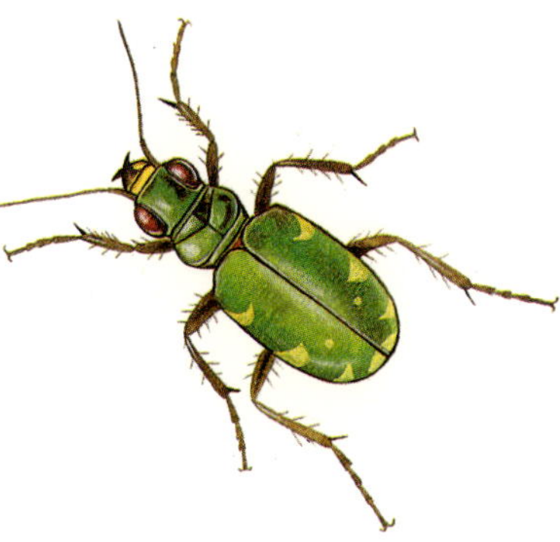

Pine Weevil

Hylobius abietis

Length: 14 mm

The pine weevil is a destructive pest of pines and other conifers. It is black with yellow-grey patches on the wing-cases and thorax. Notice the long 'snout' typical of weevils.

Furniture Beetle

Anobium punctatum

Length: 4 mm

The grubs of this tiny reddish-brown beetle are called woodworm. They burrow into furniture and house timbers and cause much damage.

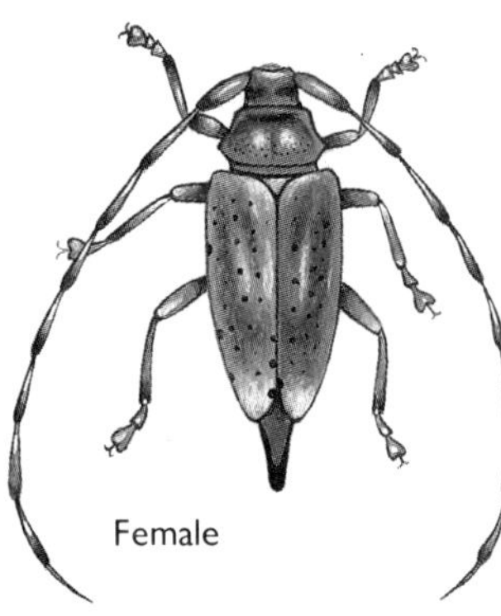

Female

Timberman

Acanthocinus aedilis

Length: 20 mm

The male of this brown long-horn beetle has antennae four times the length of its body! Those of the female are twice the length of the body. They inhabit pine forests. In Britain they are found only in the Scottish highlands.

Stag Beetle

Lucanus cervus

Length: 75 mm

This large, black beetle has huge antler-like jaws. The female is smaller and lacks the jaws.

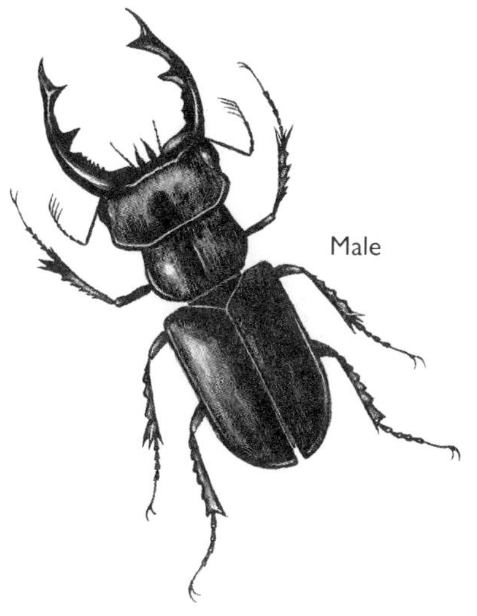

Dor Beetle

Geotrupes stercorarius

Length: 24 mm

Look for this dung beetle on summer evenings. It has a humming flight. The underside is hairy and is coloured a metallic green-violet.

Ant Beetle

Thanasimus formicarius

Length: 10 mm

This narrow-bodied beetle is found in woodland. It looks something like an ant. The thorax is orange-brown, and there are greyish bands on the wing-cases.

Bees, Ants and Wasps

★ Honey Bees

Apis mellifera

Worker: length 13 mm

The worker bees are sterile females, which cannot lay eggs. They do all the work in the beehive. They gather pollen and nectar from flowers, carrying the pollen in little sacs, or 'baskets' on the hind legs. They feed the single queen and the males, or drones.

★

Queen: length 20 mm

The main purpose of the queen is to lay eggs in cells built by the workers. Ordinary workers develop in hexagonal (six-sided) cells. New queens develop in round cells and are fed on special 'royal jelly'. Queens live for some three to four years.

★

Drone: length 15 mm

The drones, or males, do no work in the hive. Their only purpose is to mate with the queen, so that it can lay eggs. They take to the air when a new queen emerges from the hive. After mating, they die or are killed by the workers.

★ Buff-tailed Bumblebee

Bombus terrestris

Length (worker): 16 mm

Bumblebee workers, males and old queens die off each autumn. Young queens hibernate and start new colonies the following spring in nests underground. The queens (length 22 mm) have gingery tails, while those of males and workers are buff-coloured.

Common Carder Bee

Bombus agrorum

Length (worker): 18 mm

This bumblebee builds its nest above ground, often of moss and grass.

Early Mining Bee

Andrena haemorrhoa

Length: 12 mm

These look something like honey bees, but they dig shafts in the ground to lay their eggs. They often nest in lawns.

Wood Ant

Formica rufa

Length: 10 mm

The large anthills found in woodlands are made by this orange-brown ant. It cannot sting, but can bite and squirt acid at attackers. As with all ants, the males and females grow wings for their mating flight.

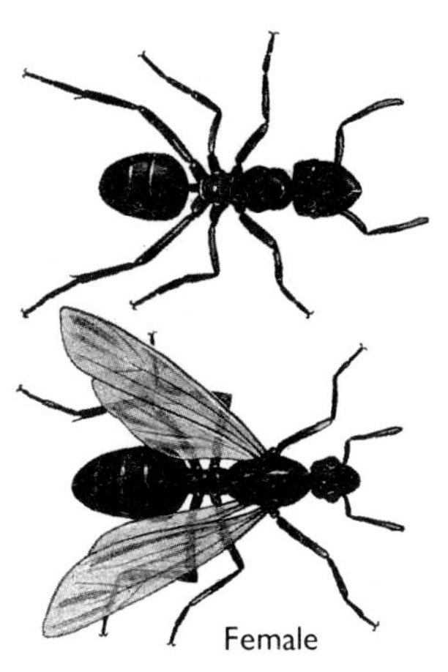

Red Ant

Myrmica ruginodis

Length: 6 mm

A common ant of the countryside, which nests under stones and in rotting tree stumps. It has sharp spines on its thorax.

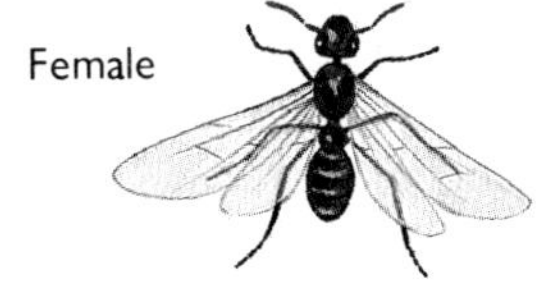

Meadow Ant

Lasius flavus

Length: 5 mm

This orange-yellow ant makes the earthy anthills found in fields. It feeds off the sweet liquid given out by aphids that live in its nest.

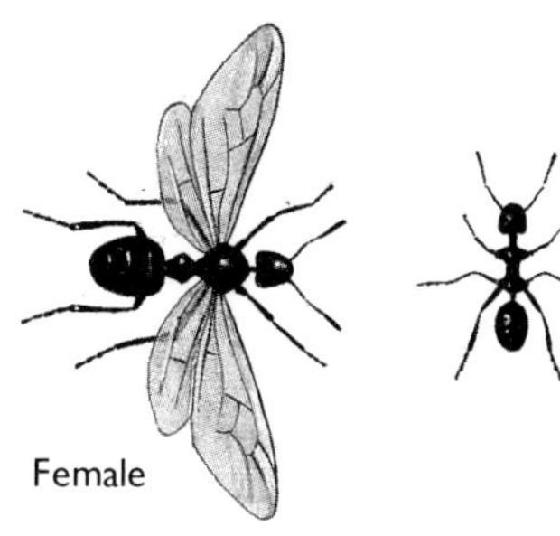

Black Ant

Lasius niger

Length: 5 mm

This is the common garden ant that also invades kitchens, searching for sugar and other sweet foods.

Common Wasp

Vespula vulgaris

Length: 20 mm

A troublesome pest that swarms around fruit trees and invades houses in the autumn. New colonies are started each year by young queens that hibernate through the winter. Tree wasps have a similar colour, but they are smaller with longer faces.

Heath Potter Wasp

Eumenes coarctata

Length: 14 mm

These wasps have narrower bodies and are mainly black with only thin yellow bands. They are so-called because they make little round 'pots' for nests from clay and tiny pebbles.

★

Hornet

Vespa crabro

Length: 30 mm

The hornet is the largest of the wasps. It is not as aggressive as the common wasp. It is found mainly in well-wooded regions, where it nests in hollow trees and sometimes in banks.

Robin's Pin-cushion Gall Wasp

Diplolepis rosae

Length: 4 mm

This is a tiny gall wasp. It lays its eggs in plant tissue, and its grubs produce hairy, red growths, or galls. They are often seen on dog roses.

★

Wall Mason Wasp

Ancistrocerus parietum

Length: 14 mm

This wasp makes a nest of mud in cracks in walls and brickwork. It also traps caterpillars for its larvae to feed on when they hatch.

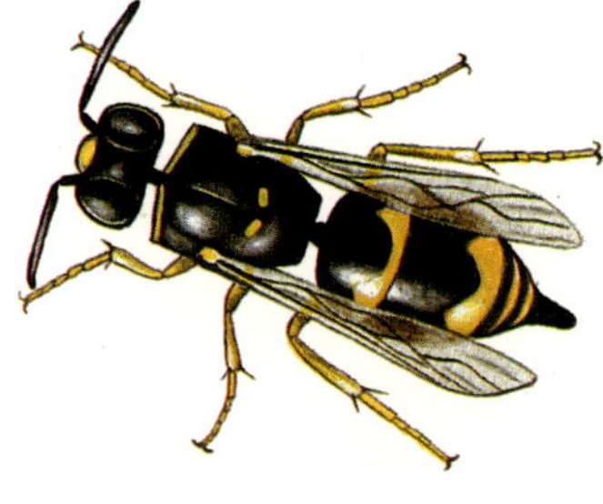

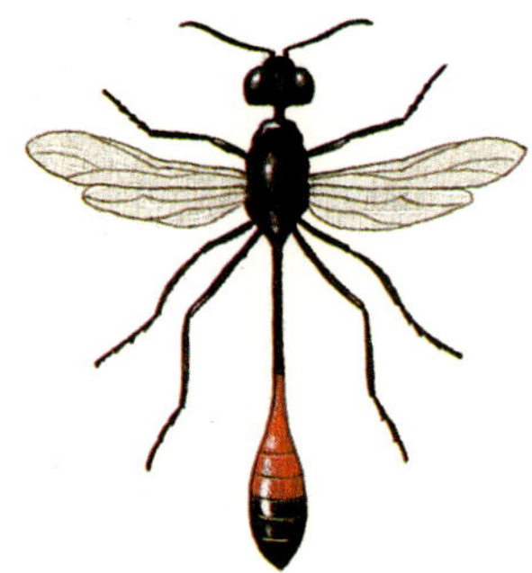

Red-banded Sand Wasp

Ammophila sabulosa

Length: 22 mm

The sand wasps are recognized by their long bodies, which are black with reddish-orange bands. They make nests in sand and also seal in caterpillars for the larvae to feed on.

★

Horn-tail Ichneumon

Rhyssa persuasoria

Length: 35 mm

This insect lays its eggs in the grubs of the giant wood wasp. To reach the grubs, it drills through wood with an ovipositor over 50 mm long.

Flies

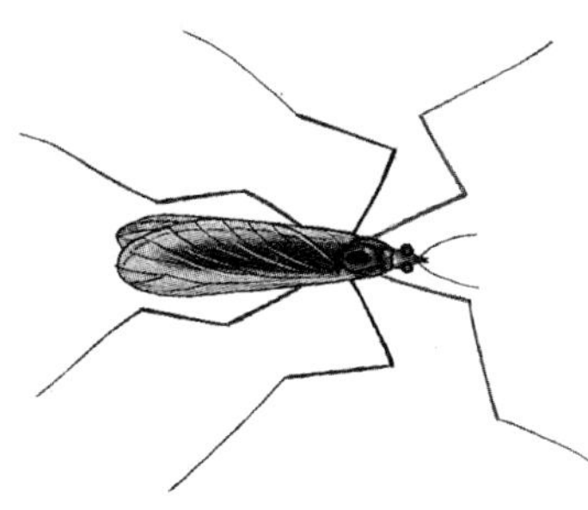

Winter Gnat

Trichocera relegationis

Span: 12 mm

These non-biting flies are so-named because they are often seen 'dancing' on winter afternoons. They are in fact around most of the year and are quite common.

Ringed Mosquito

Theobaldia annulata

Span: 18 mm

This is one of the largest and most vicious mosquitoes. The female attacks man and other mammals. It has spotted wings and white rings on its body and legs.

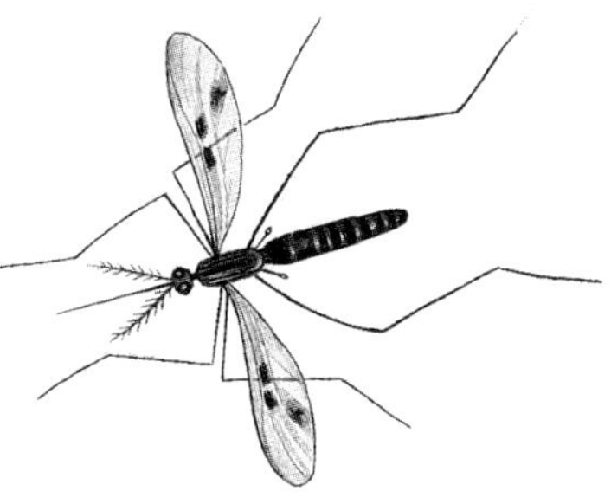

Harlequin Fly

Chironomus plumosus

Span: 18 mm

The harlequin fly is one of the largest midges. The males have feathery antennae and often swarm at dusk throughout the year. The red larvae of this midge are called bloodworms. They are found in stagnant water.

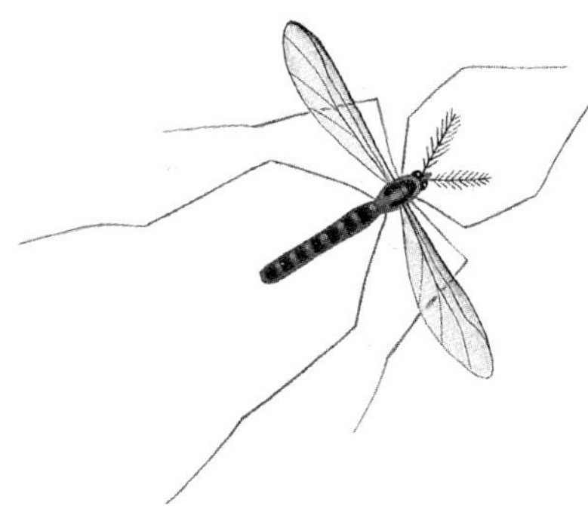

Daddy-long-legs

Tipula paludosa

Span: 45 mm

Daddy-long-legs is the name often given to crane-flies because of their long, thin legs. Notice their slim bodies and narrow wings. The greyish-brown larvae are called leatherjacks. They live in the soil and attack roots.

House Fly

Musca domestica

Span: 13 mm

This common fly is found in and around houses most of the year. It feeds on all kinds of rubbish and carries diseases.

Flesh Fly

Sarcophaga carnaria

Span: 25 mm

This is a large, black, hairy fly. It is unusual in that the eggs hatch inside the female, which then lays the larvae, or maggots.

Blow Fly

Calliphora erythrocephala

Span: 25 mm

Also called bluebottle, the blow fly is another troublesome pest, which lays its eggs in meat of any description. It is found in and around the house all through the year.

Greenbottle

Lucilia caesar

Span: 18 mm

The greenbottle is widespread in the countryside. Its brilliant metallic green colour makes it unmistakable. It feeds on the nectar of a variety of flowers.

Warble Fly

Hypoderma bovis

Span: 33 mm

This large fly lays eggs on the legs of cattle. The larvae hatch and enter the skin. They eventually find their way to the back of the animals, causing a swelling called a warble.

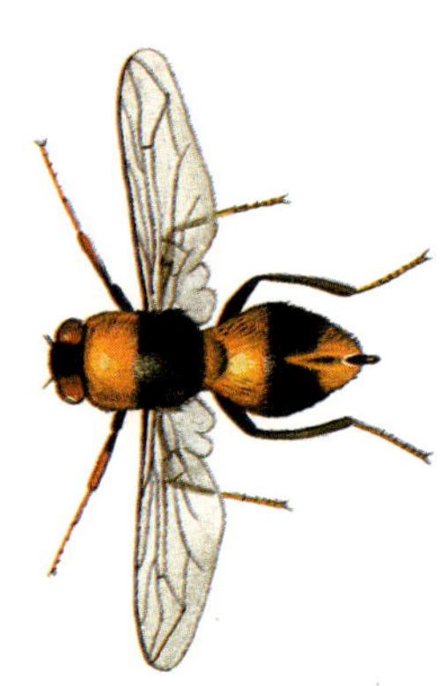

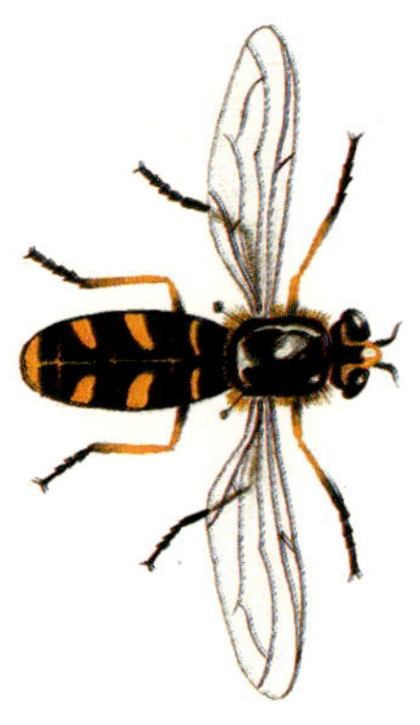

Hover Fly

Scaeva pyrastri

Span: 28 mm

This is one of the most common of several hundred species of hover flies, so-called because they often hang motionless in the air. They feed on flowers and lay eggs among greenfly and other aphids, which the larvae then eat.

Drone Fly

Eristalis tenax

Span: 25 mm

This hover fly looks like a honey bee. Its larvae live in stagnant water. They are known as rat-tailed maggots because their tails can be up to 15 cm long!

Vinegar Fly

Drosophila melanogaster

Span: 10 mm

This is also called the fruit fly. It is attracted to rotting fruit, wines and beers. People once thought that this fly turned wine into vinegar.

Other Common Insects

Bedbug

Cimex lecturarius

Length: 5 mm

This unpleasant insect is definitely unwelcome in bed because it sucks human blood. It also feeds on mice, poultry and some zoo animals. The bedbug is brown in colour and normally flattish, except when it has been gorging blood.

Toothed Shield Bug

Picromerus bidens

Length: 14 mm

This brownish-coloured bug has sharply pointed 'shoulders'. It is a useful insect because it eats caterpillars.

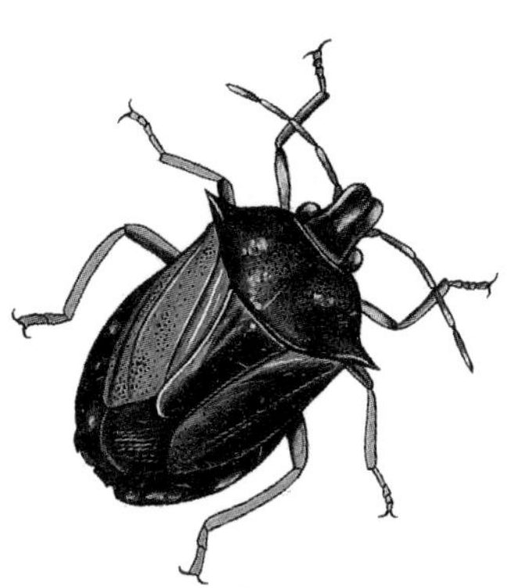

Common Froghopper

Philaenus spumarius

Length: 5 mm

The froghoppers get their name from their frog-like appearance and jumping ability. This is one of the smaller kinds. The young of this green insect makes the 'cuckoo-spit' often seen on plants.

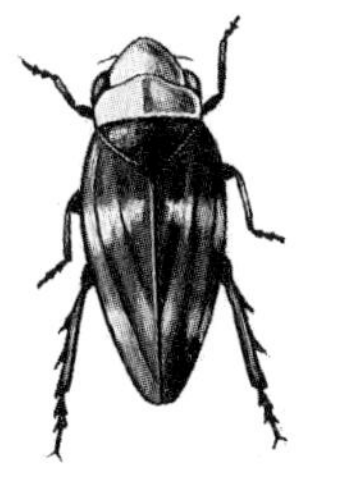

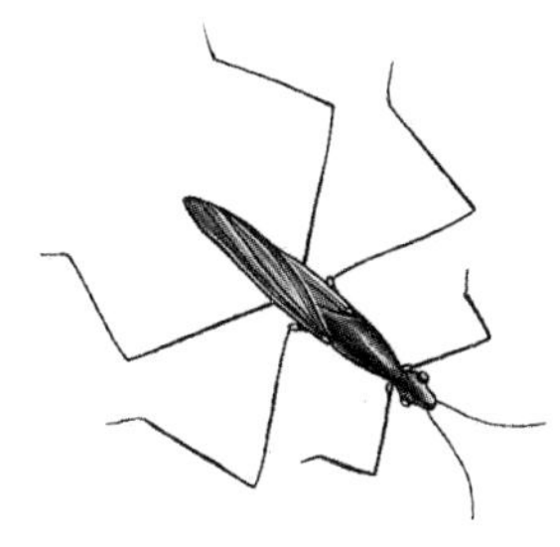

Common Pond-skater

Gerris lacustris

Length: 10 mm

This is a black water bug that 'rows' itself across the surface of water using its middle pair of legs.

Water Boatman

Notonecta glauca

Length: 15 mm

The water boatman is another common water bug. It swims on its back using its powerful hindlegs as oars. Its body is dark, with paler head and wing-cases.

Water Scorpion

Nepa cinerea

Length: 18 mm

This brown pond-dweller has a long 'tail', which is not used for stinging, like a scorpion, but for breathing. It captures insects, tadpoles and small fish in its pincer-like front legs.

Demoiselle

Agrion virgo

Length: 45 mm

This is one of the commonest damselflies. These beautiful insects are much smaller than dragonflies and, unlike them, fold their wings when resting. The demoiselle is common near rivers and streams during the summer. The male has purple-blue or green wings. The female's wings are brown.

Dragonfly

Aeshna juncea

Length: 70 mm

The male has a mainly blue body, with flecks of yellow, and blue eyes. The female has a mainly yellow or green body and dark eyes. The adult insects emerge from a dark brown nymph. There is no pupa stage.

Mayfly

Ephemera danica

Length: 13 mm

The adult mayfly lives for only three or four days. Notice its tail, which is made up of three very long threads. Mayflies are loved by fish, especially trout.

Green Lacewing

Chrysopa 7-punctata

Length: 15 mm

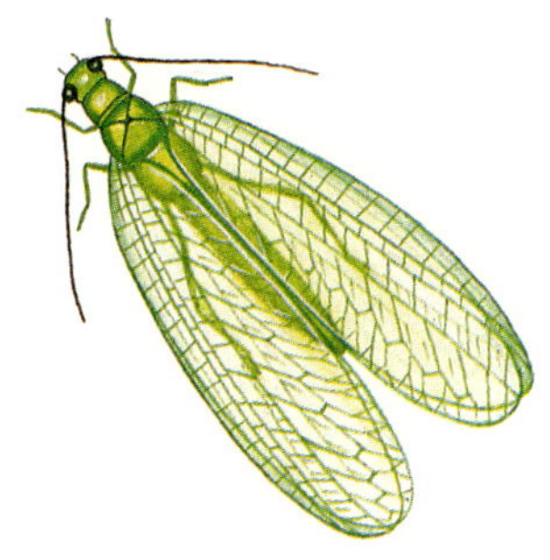

This common lacewing has delicate, green wings, with gold-coloured eyes. Like other lacewings, it feeds on aphids. When attacked, it gives off a foul-smelling liquid from stink glands.

Great Green Grasshopper

Tettigonia viridissima

Length: 55 mm

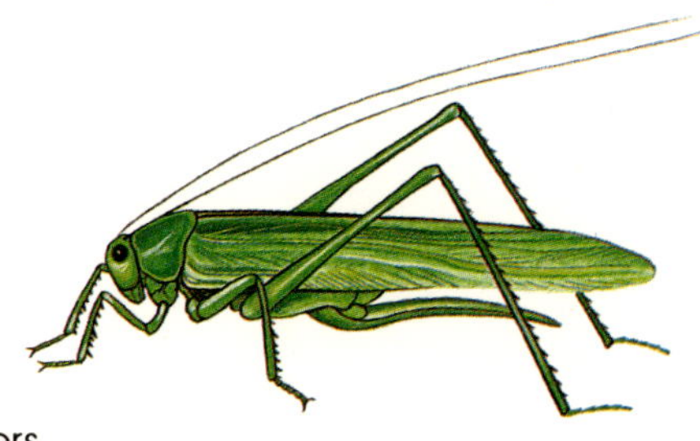

This is a long-horned grasshopper, or bush cricket. True grasshoppers have short antennae. It is found in thick vegetation.

House Cricket

Acheta domesticus

Length: 25 mm

A brownish insect found in old buildings, where its shrill 'chirps' can often be heard. It is the males that make the noise. They do so by rubbing a toothed 'file' on the right forewing against the rear of the left hindwing. Crickets have their 'ears' on their front legs.

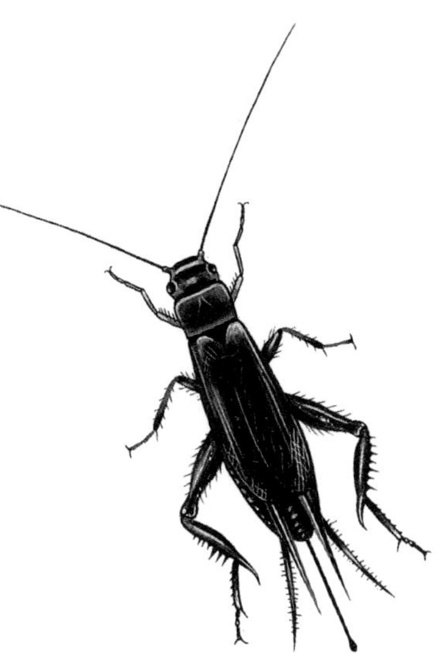

Common Cockroach

Blatta orientalis

Length: 22 mm

This black insect pest has a broad body and long antennae. It is found in warm places, especially where food is being prepared. It hides during the daytime, and feeds at night. The lighter coloured American cockroach can also sometimes be found. It can grow nearly twice as big as the common cockroach.

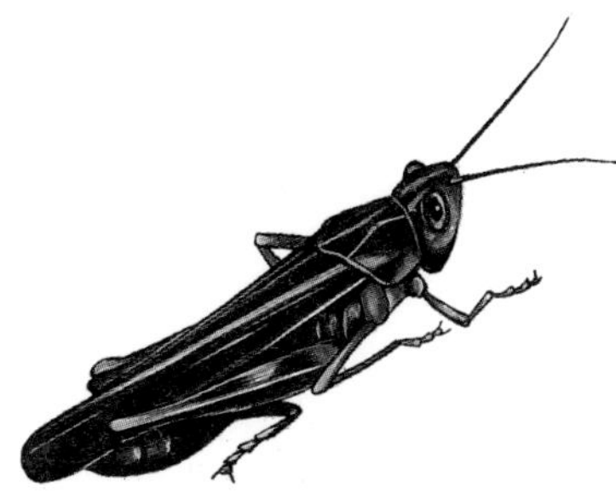

Common Grasshopper

Chorthippus brunneus

Length: 22 mm

This true grasshopper has the typical short antennae. It likes fields and dry places, and is brownish in colour.

Silverfish

Lepisma saccharina

Length: 10 mm

A silvery-white, wingless insect found in most kitchens, where it feeds on starchy scraps. It has three fine bristles on its tail.

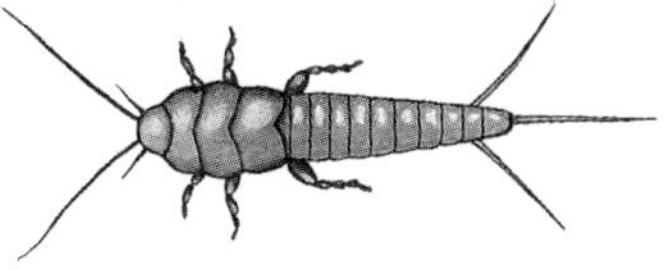

Common Earwig

Forficula auricularia

Length: 14 mm

This familiar brown insect is so-called because it was thought to like getting into people's ears. Fortunately, this is not true. The female looks after the young until they can fend for themselves.

Index